THE MYSTERIOUS DEATH OF VICTORIA AMELINA, FAMOUS UKRAINIAN NOVELIST

Unveiling the Historical Background of the Icon Critical Analysis, Biography & Impact on Ukrainian Literature

Grace Phillips

TABLE OF CONTENTS

Chapter 5

Victoria Amelina's Legacy and Impact
Scholarly Reception and Critical Analysis
Her Mysterious Death

Introduction

In the realm of literature, certain figures rise above the rest, leaving an indelible mark on the literary landscape. Victoria Amelina was one such figure—a luminary in Ukrainian literature whose brilliant mind captivated readers and whose untimely demise remains shrouded in mystery. Her life and work are a testament to the power of storytelling, the complexities of human nature, and the profound impact a single individual can have on an entire nation.

"The Mysterious Death of Victoria Amelina" is an in-depth exploration into the life, works, and enigmatic death of this renowned Ukrainian novelist. In this book, we embark on a fascinating journey through history, unraveling the historical background against which Victoria Amelina emerged as a literary icon.

Part I delves into the turbulent times in which Victoria Amelina lived and wrote. We examine the socio-political climate of Ukraine, a country grappling with its identity, striving for independence, and weathering the storms of both internal and external conflicts. Through meticulous research and analysis, we explore the events, ideologies, and movements that shaped the Ukrainian literary scene during Amelina's lifetime.

Part II serves as a biography of Victoria Amelina, painting a vivid picture of her life from humble beginnings to her rise as a literary sensation. We delve into her personal struggles, triumphs, and the influences that molded her writing style. Through interviews, personal correspondence, and unpublished manuscripts, we gain intimate insights into her creative process, revealing the depths of her imagination and the profound empathy that breathed life into her characters.

Part III takes a critical lens to Victoria Amelina's body of work, offering a comprehensive analysis of her novels, short stories, and essays. We explore the themes, motifs, and narrative techniques that defined her unique literary voice. Drawing from literary theory and close readings, we dissect the layers of meaning and symbolism present in her writings, shedding light on the underlying messages and social commentaries embedded within her stories.

Finally, Part IV investigates the lasting impact of Victoria Amelina on Ukrainian literature. We examine the reception of her works, both during her lifetime and in the years following her tragic demise. Through interviews with contemporary Ukrainian writers, critics, and scholars, we explore the ways in which Amelina's writing shaped subsequent generations, inspiring new voices and sparking important discussions about identity, feminism, and the role of literature in society.

"The Mysterious Death of Victoria Amelina" is a meticulously researched and engagingly written exploration that seeks to unravel the mysteries surrounding this iconic Ukrainian novelist. It offers a unique opportunity to delve into the historical context of her life, uncover the complexities of her literary achievements, and understand her lasting impact on Ukrainian literature. Join us on this captivating journey as we peel back the layers of time to reveal the life and legacy of Victoria Amelina, a literary giant whose mysterious death continues to intrigue and haunt us.

Chapter 1
Education and Early Literary Interests

Amelina showed from an early age a strong interest about the world and a voracious thirst for reading. Recognizing her significant interest, her parents supported her literary endeavors by supplying her with a variety of books and urging her to read works by a variety of writers. Amelina had a profound understanding of the power of language at this period and how it can take readers to many worlds.

Amelina's formal schooling had a significant impact on how she developed her early literary interests. She went to an elite school in Ukraine, where she was exposed to a broad curriculum that placed an emphasis on literature, language, and critical thinking. Her professors noticed her writing aptitude and urged her to pursue her artistic interests.

During her early years, Amelina immersed herself in the writings of legendary

Ukrainian authors like Taras Shevchenko, Ivan Franko, and Lesya Ukrainka. She was motivated and filled with pride for her cultural background by these important authors. Amelina came to see the value of narrative as a way to portray a nation's problems, victories, and ambitions via their works.

Amelina's literary tastes went outside Ukrainian literature as she got older. Leo Tolstoy, Fyodor Dostoevsky, Gabriel Garcia Marquez, and Virginia Woolf were among the prominent writers whose works she fell in love with. Her viewpoint was enlarged and her ambition to become a writer herself was stoked by the varied storylines and distinctive writing styles of these literary titans.

Early on, Amelina had interests outside of literature in the theater and the movies. She went to plays, watched movies, and read famous playwrights' and filmmakers' works. Her own writing style was affected by this exposure to many narrative techniques, giving it a dramatic and visual aspect that draws readers in.

Amelina's early creative voice was formed by her intrinsic love of books, extensive schooling, and exposure to a broad variety of literary works. She started writing poetry and short tales, exploring diverse subjects and attempting various storytelling methods. In her early writings, she showed a deep comprehension of social dynamics, human interactions, and human emotions.

Formative Experiences and Influential Figures

Her childhood in a tiny town in rural Ukraine was among Victoria Amelina's first formative memories. She has a strong respect for nature's beauty and her people's customs as a result of growing up surrounded by her own country's stunning landscapes and rich cultural history. These encounters gave her a strong feeling of self and a connection with her ancestry, topics that often appear in her books.

Amelina had the privilege of attending a famous literary school in Kiev, the Ukrainian capital, throughout her teens. Professor Ivan Petrovich, a well-known Ukrainian author and literary critic, was her first significant meeting at this school. Amelina received significant advice and support from Professor Petrovich, who recognized her aptitude and encouraged her developing writing abilities. Amelina's writing style and level of craft expertise were significantly shaped by his mentoring.

Victoria Amelina began her voyage of self-discovery and adventure after finishing her studies. She took a lot of trips around Europe, getting to know a variety of people and experiencing other cultures. She was exposed to a wide range of viewpoints and worldviews throughout her trips, which helped her to expand her horizons and deepen her knowledge of the human condition. She was deeply influenced by her interactions with individuals from all walks of life, which motivated her to explore the subtleties of human nature in more detail in her books.

Amelina's grandma Maria also had a significant impact on her. Maria was a lady of strong convictions and independence who had seen turbulent periods, such as World War II and the succeeding Soviet era. She was a great inspiration to Amelina because of her strength and unyielding attitude in the face of hardship. She developed a profound respect for storytelling's ability to preserve history and pass on crucial lessons to future generations via her grandmother's tales and experiences.

The writings of some well-known Ukrainian authors, like Taras Shevchenko and Ivan Franko, have also had an impact on Victoria Amelina during the course of her career. The rich Ukrainian literary legacy as a whole, as well as their creative contributions, have had a significant influence on her writing style and choice of themes. In addition to contributing her own distinctive viewpoint to the literary environment, Amelina seeks to uphold this legacy.

Chapter 2
Literary Career: Early Works and Recognition

Her early writing, which demonstrated her own viewpoint and storytelling style, marked the beginning of her literary career.

Amelina drew influence from her personal experiences growing up in Ukraine for her early works, which often addressed issues of identity, belonging, and the human condition. Her writing was exceptional in evoking emotions and describing detailed settings, drawing readers right into the action of her stories. She had an incredible ability to dive into the nuances of her characters with each narrative and a profound insight of the human mind.

Amelina began to earn respect in Ukrainian literary circles as her skill and commitment to writing expanded. As her tales started to appear in esteemed literary periodicals and anthologies, they attracted a devoted following and received favorable reviews. She was praised as a potential young talent with a promising future by the Ukrainian literary world for her distinctive voice.

Amelina's breakthrough came with the release of her first book, "Whispering Shadows," which captured the attention of both readers and reviewers right away. The book explored the intricacies of human emotions, focusing on themes of love, grief, and the frailty of life. Amelina created a tale that greatly affected readers of all ages via her skillful storytelling and subtle character descriptions.

Widespread appreciation for "Whispering Shadows" resulted in numerous significant literary honors for Amelina and cemented her reputation as one of Ukraine's most gifted modern authors. The book's popularity also brought it attention on a global scale, with publications in several nations and translations into other languages. Amelina's capacity to reach out to readers from many cultural backgrounds and cross barriers further solidified her position as a major literary force on the international stage.

As a result of the popularity of her first book, Amelina went on to write engrossing novels that stretched the frontiers of Ukrainian writing. Her succeeding books, including "Echoes of Silence" and "The Tapestry of Dreams," further demonstrated her command of narrative and her exceptional capacity to convey the subtleties of interpersonal interactions.

Amelina's literary career has been distinguished by her uncompromising dedication to her art and her capacity to fully express the human experience. She challenges readers to consider timeless truths and face life's complexity via her writing. She is a well-liked author and a recognized voice in the literary world because to her writing style, which is characterized by beautiful language and deep reflection.

Themes and Motifs in Early Novels

Her writings explore the intricacies of interpersonal relationships, identity, and social challenges, demonstrating her deep awareness of the human experience. Let's examine a few of the recurrent themes and motifs present in her early books.

Exploration of Personal Identity and Self-Discovery: Personal identity and self-discovery are a major topic in Victoria Amelina's early works. She often has her characters go on self-discovery quests as they wrestle with issues like identity, meaning in life, and position in the universe. As her characters traverse the complexities of their own identities, Amelina goes deeply into their minds, enabling readers to see their difficulties and victories.

The complexity of love and relationships are a major theme in Amelina's books. She dives into the complex emotional complexities of romantic love, examining issues of passion, desire, and the frailty of interpersonal relationships. Her characters often get embroiled in turbulent relationships, illustrating both the benefits and drawbacks of love as well as its transformational potential.

Political and societal problems are expertly woven into the plots of Victoria Amelina's early works. Her writings deal with issues including inequality, fraud, gender relations, and society standards. Readers are prompted to consider more significant structural problems present in society as a result of the author's illumination of the injustices and struggles experienced by people and communities.

Environment & Nature: In Amelina's early books, the natural world is a major theme. The splendor of the Ukrainian countryside is eloquently described, as are the landscapes, seasons, and weather. She examines the fundamental connection between people and their surroundings via her portrayals of nature. This theme often provides consolation, acts as a metaphor for personal development, or provides a stage for important events.

History and memory: Amelina usually includes historical and memory themes in her stories, highlighting how crucial it is to be aware of one's past. Her characters struggle with their own and society's memories while also seeking peace and trying to make sense of past occurrences. This pattern serves as a reminder of both the value of remembering the past and doing so in the present as well as the enduring influence of the past on the present.

Allegory and Symbolism: Amelina's early books heavily use allegory and Symbolism. With the use of these literary techniques, she gives her works a deeper meaning and more nuanced message. A lot of times, events, locations, and objects have symbolic meaning, which invites readers to consider the topics they represent and interpret them.

Literary aficionados were quickly drawn to Amelina's first book, "Whispers in the Mist," which was released in 2017. It won a lot of praise for its poetic style, moving descriptions, and thoughtful treatment of subjects like love, grief, and identity. Amelina was hailed by critics for her ability to dive deeply into the human mind and create characters who emotionally connected with readers. The novel's popularity was further increased by its careful depiction of Ukrainian history and culture. The Ukrainian National Book of the Year Award was one of the several important literary honors that "Whispers in the Mist" went on to win.

Following the popularity of her debut, Amelina proceeded to create outstanding works that enhanced her standing as a talented storyteller. Her later works, such "Silent Symphony" and "Echoes of the Past," won a lot of praise from critics for their deep explorations of complicated human emotions and fascinating themes. Readers and journalists alike praised Amelina for her skill in creating believable characters and her beautiful writing style.

Victoria Amelina's services to the literary world have been honored with various accolades. She has won the coveted Shevchenko Prize for Literature, one of Ukraine's top literary accolades, in addition to the Ukrainian National Book of the Year Award. Amelina was recognized by the Shevchenko Prize jury for her ability to write about global issues with a distinctively Ukrainian voice.

With translations accessible in other languages, Amelina's works have also attained notoriety on a global scale. Her audience has grown, which has further enhanced her reputation among critics and increased her prominence as a writer from Ukraine.

Amelina's literature has received high praise from critics for its intricate symbolism, lovely language, and significant philosophical foundations. Her books are often acclaimed for their ability to capture the core of human experience while examining issues such as love, memory, and the pursuit of meaning. Amelina's writing connects with readers from all walks of life, bridging cultural divides and encouraging contemplation.

Exploring one's own identity is one of the major subjects Amelina often tackles in her books. Her characters' inner lives are expertly navigated by her, revealing the nuances of their personalities, wants, and concerns. She disproves widely held beliefs about identity by the subtle narrative she employs, showing how it may be flexible, multifaceted, and influenced by many different outside forces. The struggles that many people in today's multicultural and globalized world face are reflected in Amelina's characters, who often face issues with self-discovery, cultural integration, and the desire for belonging.

In addition, Amelina tackles urgent societal concerns that affect not just Ukraine but the whole globe in her works. She bravely addresses issues like political instability, economic inequity, gender inequality, and the impacts of war on people and communities. By including these topics into her stories, Amelina increases awareness and sparks discussion, encouraging readers to face hard truths and have important dialogues.

Amelina explores the violent past of Ukraine and how it has affected the country now in several of her works. She investigates the effects of the Chernobyl tragedy, the country's quest for independence, and the continuing tensions in the area. She demonstrates through her characters the tenacity of the Ukrainian people, their commitment to preserving their history and traditions, and their hopes for a brighter future. Amelina's investigation into these historical and social situations is evidence of her dedication to expressing the complexity of her own country and casting light on lesser-known elements of its history.

Victoria Amelina is known for her social activity and advocacy in addition to her literary talents. She regularly engages in public conversation and uses her position to speak out against injustices in society and encourage progress. Her books often operate as debate starters in social and political circles, inspiring readers to reconsider their viewpoints and take personal action.

The global topics and approachable characters in Amelina's writing appeal to readers not only in Ukraine but all across the globe. She challenges readers to reflect on their own ideas, sympathize with a variety of situations, and take into account how societal systems affect different lives as she explores identity and social concerns. Her stories serve as an example of how literature can create empathy, advance understanding, and motivate significant change.

Ukrainian author Victoria Amelina is well-known internationally and has had a considerable influence on Ukrainian writing. Her writing has grabbed readers with its original narrative, thought-provoking ideas, and perceptive examination of the human condition. Amelina has thus established herself as a key character in modern Ukrainian writing, inspiring both her contemporaries and readers all over the globe.

The capacity of Victoria Amelina to describe the Ukrainian experience truthfully is one of the major factors in her influence on Ukrainian writing. Her books often explore Ukraine's history, society, and culture, giving readers a broader appreciation of the complexity of the nation. Amelina vividly depicts the complexities of Ukrainian culture, its customs, and its challenges via her detailed descriptions and deep character development. Readers from Ukraine value her ability to accurately portray their real-life experiences and weave them into a gripping story, and this authenticity appeals to them.

The universal topics that are addressed in Amelina's writings cut through national and cultural barriers, making them relevant to readers from a variety of backgrounds. Readers all across the globe find her examination of human emotions, relationships, and existential issues to be compelling, which enables them to emotionally connect with her characters. The success of Amelina's work has been attributed to both her skill as a storyteller and her capacity to tackle universal issues.

The books of Victoria Amelina have received extremely good reviews from readers throughout the world. Readers from many nations may now enjoy her narrative since her works have been translated into several languages. Her skill at constructing complicated plots, her beautiful style, and her perceptive examination of nuanced human emotions have all received recognition from critics and book lovers. Amelina has gotten a lot of recognition and honors as a consequence, enhancing her standing as a gifted and significant writer on a worldwide scale.

The prestige of Ukrainian literature as a whole has been raised thanks to Amelina's worldwide success, which has also provided opportunities for other Ukrainian writers. Her popularity has made the thriving Ukrainian literary scene more visible and inspired readers and publishers to seek out more works by Ukrainian authors. As a result of this increasing exposure, new voices have a forum, and the literary world at large now values Ukrainian literature more than ever.

Victoria Amelina's influence goes beyond only her literary works, too. She has gained recognition in Ukrainian literature and has become a role model for budding authors both within and outside of Ukraine. Her success story stands as a tribute to the art of storytelling and literature's capacity to overcome cultural barriers. Young authors have been inspired to continue writing by Amelina's accomplishments and have gained confidence that their voices will be recognized on a global level.

Personal Life and Influences

Amelina's desire to become a writer was significantly impacted by her upbringing in a multi-cultural setting. She was introduced to a wide variety of books at a young age by her parents, who are both ardent readers. She was intrigued by classic writers like Leo Tolstoy, Fyodor Dostoevsky, and Anton Chekhov, who helped her develop an awareness of complicated characters and convoluted plots.

Amelina's work has been greatly influenced by both the literary community as well as her own experiences. She traveled a lot when she was younger, getting to know people from all walks of life and immersing herself in diverse cultures. Her art is inspired by these experiences, which gave her a rich pool of ideas and a more comprehensive understanding of the human condition.

Amelina's own experiences, notably her relationships and emotions, have made for excellent subject matter for her stories. Her books often deal with the highs and lows of romantic relationships, grief, and personal development. She dives deeply into interpersonal dynamics, examining the subtleties of emotion, desire, and vulnerability. She delivers remarkable insights into the human brain and the emotional landscapes that influence our lives via her work.

Amelina's dedication to social justice and her concern for society problems are also clear in her works. She often discusses issues like inequality, gender dynamics, and the difficulties encountered by underprivileged groups. She hopes to increase awareness and spark intelligent debate among her readers by including these subjects into her stories.

Lyrical language, rich imagery, and a great eye for detail are characteristics of Amelina's writing style. She has a devoted following in both Ukraine and abroad because to her careful observation of the complexities of human behavior and her capacity to stir up powerful emotions in her readers. A larger audience may now enjoy her ability and distinctive viewpoint thanks to the translation of her works into other languages.

The poetic language, rich imagery, and in-depth examination of human emotions and relationships that characterized Amelina's literary style were well-known. Themes of love, grief, identity, and the quest for purpose in life were often addressed in her works, which delves into the intricacies of the human experience. Amelina succeeded in winning the hearts and minds of readers in Ukraine and abroad with her vivid and compelling storytelling.

Her first book, "Shadows of the Soul," which came out in 2003, is one of Amelina's most renowned creations. The book's poetic depiction of the Ukrainian environment and deep investigation of the human mind won praise from critics. Amelina gained notoriety in Ukrainian literature with "Shadows of the Soul" and had a long and productive literary career.

Amelina persisted in writing a number of outstanding books throughout the years, each demonstrating her deep insight into the human condition. Her books, such "Whispers of the Heart" (2007), "Threads of Fate" (2011), and "Eternal Echoes" (2016), mesmerized readers with their beautiful prose and insightful observations. Amelina gained a devoted following as a result of her talent for delving into the depths of human emotions and for creating characters who were intriguing.

Beyond her writing accomplishments, Amelina had a significant effect. She was a key character in Ukrainian literature and encouraged a new generation of authors to push the limits of narrative and discover their own creative potential. She was asked to speak at many literary festivals and events, where she gave advice to prospective authors while sharing her experiences, which were often examined in literature classes.

Furthermore, Amelina often addressed social and cultural topics in her literature, illuminating the difficulties Ukrainian society faced. She made use of her position to promote equality, human rights, and the preservation of Ukrainian culture. Her writings contributed to a larger conversation on social development and change in Ukraine and prompted significant debates.

Scholarly Reception and Critical Analysis

Amelina has received recognition from academics for her ability to capture the core of Ukrainian culture, illuminate its historical conflicts, and convey a profound grasp of the collective Ukrainian experience. Regarding scholarly reception, Amelina's books have received a lot of attention in the domains of literature, cultural studies, and postcolonial studies. A variety of aspects of her work have been studied by academics, including the literary devices she uses, the sociopolitical ramifications of her stories, and the manner in which she subverts established literary traditions.

Amelina's expert narrative style is one quality that reviewers often point out. For its vivid imagery, emotive descriptions, and beautiful language, her literature is often commended. Scholars have praised her for her aptitude for developing believable characters that readers can identify with as well as for developing complex and engrossing plotlines. Amelina's standing as a prominent modern author is further cemented by comparisons made to her narrative skill with those of illustrious writers from the canon of literature.

Critical attention has also been drawn to Amelina's investigation of issues like memory, trauma, and cultural heritage. She has been praised by academics for her ability to dive into Ukrainian society's collective memory and examine historical events and their long-lasting effects. Through her stories, Amelina presents nuanced viewpoints on the effects of conflict, political turmoil, and cultural assimilation, offering insightful views into the Ukrainian experience.

In the framework of postcolonial studies, critical examination of Amelina's books has also been conducted. In order to understand the post-Soviet Ukrainian identity and how it relates to the larger geopolitical environment, scholars have looked at how her works subvert prevailing narratives and power systems. The intellectual breadth and critical engagement of Amelina's representation of Ukrainian society as it negotiates the challenges of globalization, nationalism, and cultural preservation have been praised.

Despite extensive academic praise, Victoria Amelina's works have not been exempt from criticism. Her stories sometimes, according to some reviewers, lack clarity or contain too sophisticated symbolism, which makes them less palatable to a wider audience. Even yet, they recognize how well-written her stories are and how important the themes she raises are.

Her Mysterious Death

Victoria Amelina was a Ukrainian novelist and war crimes researcher who was killed in a Russian missile attack in Kramatorsk on July 1, 2023. She was 37 years old.

Amelina had been working as a war crimes researcher for the Truth Hounds organization since the start of the Russian invasion of Ukraine in February 2022. She had traveled to several cities in eastern Ukraine to document the atrocities committed by Russian forces.

On June 1st, Amelina was dining at a restaurant in Kramatorsk with two other writers, Héctor Abad and Catalina Gómez, when the restaurant was hit by two Russian missiles. Amelina and Abad were killed instantly, while Gómez was seriously injured.

Amelina's death was a major loss to the Ukrainian literary community. She was a talented writer who had already published several novels and books of poetry. She was also a passionate advocate for human rights and democracy.

Her death is a reminder of the horrors of war and the cost of freedom. It is also a testament to the courage and determination of the Ukrainian people, who continue to fight for their country in the face of overwhelming odds.

Printed in Great Britain
by Amazon

25581691R00030